What's Living in Your Backyard?

Andrew Solway

Heinemann Library
Chicago, Illinois

© 2004 Heinemann Library
a division of Reed Elsevier, Inc.
Chicago, Illinois

Customer Service 888-454-2279
Visit our website at www.heinemannlibrary.com

Designed by David Poole and Paul Myerscough
Illustrations by Geoff Ward
Originated by Dot Gradations
Printed and bound in China by South China Printing Company

09 08 07 06 05 04
10 9 8 7 6 5 4 3 2 1

Library of Congress Cataloging-in-Publication Data
Solway, Andrew.
    What's living in your backyard? / Andrew Solway.
      v. cm. -- (Hidden life)
    Contents: Taking a closer look -- Spidery sap suckers -- Roundworms -- Leaf spot, mildew, canker and blight -- Under-ground partnerships -- Microlife in the soil -- The decomposers -- Microscopic grazers -- Creating compost -- Water life -- More water life.
    ISBN 1-4034-4843-4 (hc : lib. bdg.) -- ISBN 1-4034-5482-5 (pb.)
    1. Soil microbiology--Juvenile literature. 2. Lawns--Juvenile lit-erature.   [1. Microbiology.]   I. Title. II. Series.
    QR111.S677 2004
    579'.17554--dc22

                                2003018007

Acknowledgments
The author and publishers are grateful to the following for permission to reproduce copyright material: pp. 4, 20b Liz Eddison; p. 5t Science Photo Library (R. Maisonneuve, Publiphoto Diffusion), p. 5b (Astrid and Hanns Freider Michler), p. 6, 13, 27 (Dr Jeremy Burgess), p. 7 (Martin Dohrn), p. 8t (Ken Eward), p. 9 (James King-Holmes), pp. 10t, 11 (Andrew Syred), pp. 10b, 12t, 13t (Vaughan Fleming), pp. 15, 16 (David Scharf), p. 17b (Microfield Scientific Ltd), p. 18 (Eye of Science), pp. 19b, 21b, 23 (Manfred Kage),
p. 22t (Georgette Douwma), p. 22b (Eric Grave), p. 24 (Dr David Patterson), pp. 25t, 25b (John Walsh); pp. 8, 14 Holt Studio International; p. 17t Alamy Images; p. 19t Science Photo Library; p. 20t Corbis (Sally A. Morgan, Ecoscene).

Cover photograph of the head of a springtail, reproduced with permission of Science Photo Library/David Scharf.

Our thanks to Dr. Philip Parrillo, entomologist at the Field Museum in Chicago, for his comments in the preparation of this book.

Some words are shown in bold, **like this.** You can find out what they mean by looking in the glossary.

Contents

Taking a Closer Look 4

Spidery Sap Suckers 6

Roundworms 8

Plant Parasites 10

Underground Partnerships 12

Microlife in the Soil 14

The Decomposers 16

Microscopic Grazers 18

Creating Compost 20

Water Life .22

More Water Life 24

Two-in-One Creatures 26

Table of Sizes 28

Glossary *30*

More Books to Read *31*

Index *32*

Many of the photos in this book were taken using a microscope. In the captions you may see a number that tells you how much they have been enlarged. For example, a photo marked "(x200)" is about 200 times bigger than in real life.

Taking a Closer Look

A garden has life everywhere. Flowers, shrubs, and trees grow in the soil. Bees and other insects visit the flowers. Birds and mammals eat the insects and plants. Sometimes there is a pond, with tadpoles and frogs. But if you look closer, you will find another whole world—hidden life that is visible only through a magnifying glass or a microscope.

Plant residents

If you look at your plants through a magnifying glass, you might spot tiny spiderlike creatures called **mites.** They live by sucking sap from plants. Even smaller are the tiny **roundworms** that live on most plants. Some of them live on the plant surface, while others burrow into the leaves or roots.

The plants in the garden depend on microbes and other tiny creatures that enrich the soil.

With a microscope, you will be able to find **microbes** on the surface of plants. Many of them do the plant no harm, but some can cause plant diseases. The most harmful microbes are **fungi,** which are relatives of mushrooms.

Living dirt

If you dig into the soil in the garden, you will probably uncover earthworms, centipedes, beetles, and other minibeasts. But there are a whole range of microbes that live in the soil as well. They do an important

job, breaking down dead plant and animal material into useful **nutrients.** These nutrients become part of the soil and help plants to grow. The microbes themselves are food for the soil

A light microscope is easy to use, and it is possible to look at tiny, live creatures.

Electron microscopes are expensive and complicated to use. But they have helped scientists to get a close look at even the tiniest bacteria.

minibeasts, which in turn get eaten by bigger animals such as birds, moles, mice, and shrews.

MICROSCOPES

The reason we know so much about the hidden life in a garden is because scientists have used microscopes to study microbes. A light microscope—the kind of microscope that you might have used at school or at home—can magnify things up to 1,800 times. But to get   close look at really tiny things such as bacteria, you need an electron microscope.   n electron microscope can magnify objects up to 500,000 times.

Spidery Sap Suckers

Hold a piece of white paper under a plant in your garden. Now give the stem a sharp tap. Some little specks will fall onto the paper. The specks may be bits of dirt and dust, but if they start to crawl around, they are probably spider mites.

Mites are relatives of spiders. They have a roundish body, a small head, and eight legs. Most are barely visible to the naked eye. The mites that live on plants spin webs, which is why they are called spider mites.

↺ *Red mites (x330) are pests of many crops. They have no eyes. Instead, the sensory hairs on their body tell them about the outside world.*

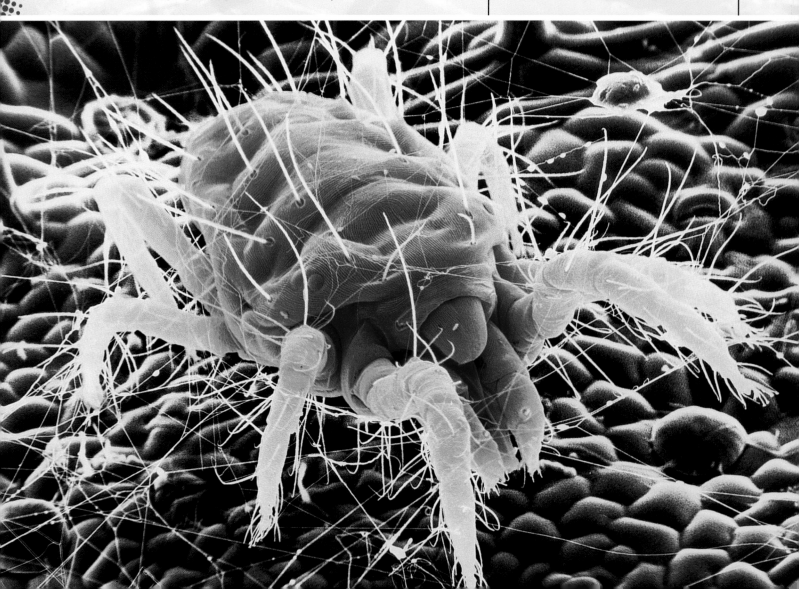

lifestyle

Spider mites have two thin, needle-sharp structures called **stylets,** which they use to make holes in leaf **cells.** They then suck up sap from the cells.

A female mite lives for four to six weeks and produces up to 150 eggs. If it is warm, the eggs can become adults in just a week, so mite numbers can explode during a hot summer.

When they first hatch, young mites are called **larvae.** They have six legs rather than eight. After a few days the larvae **molt** and become **nymphs.** Nymphs have eight legs. After two more molts and another five or six days, the nymphs become adults.

Fight mites with mites

Spider mites are plant pests because they damage many of the crops we grow. They can stunt the growth of a plant, or even kill it.

One way to control spider mites is to use other mites. Some kinds of mites are

predators on spider mites. They eat the spider mites and their eggs, keeping the numbers of these pests low.

The orange mite is a predator that is attacking a spider mite.

WARM AND COOL MITES

Some mites like hot weather and do best in places with warm summers. Females born in the fall spend the winter in a resting state (a kind of **hibernation).** In spring the females become active and lay eggs.

Other spider mites prefer cooler conditions. They are most active in spring and fall and rest during the summer and winter.

Roundworms

Most gardens have plenty of earthworms. But there are also millions of much smaller worms called **roundworms.** Roundworms are a fraction of a millimeter long, and their bodies are transparent. Some are **parasites** on plants, but there are also millions of free-living roundworms in the soil.

stylet

This photo of a plant-eating roundworm, shows its sharp **stylet.**

Root-eating roundworms often cause diseases in crops. This pea plant has knots caused by roundworms feeding on its roots.

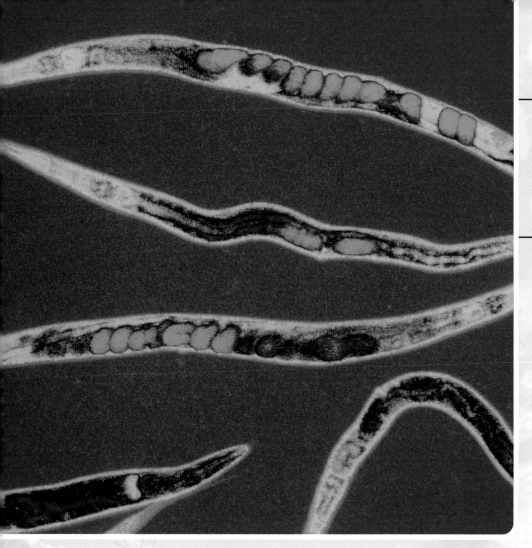

Some roundworms live on the upper parts of plants, but many more live on the roots. Some kinds burrow into the root, then settle down and begin to eat. As they eat, they swell and become pear-shaped or round. Often the root around them swells, too, producing a thickening called a knot.

A roundworm's life

A roundworm's body is a simple tube. Most of the inside of this tube is taken up with the gut. Muscles run along the length of the body, but there are no muscles running in other directions, so a roundworm can move its body only from side to side. The head of a roundworm has a few tiny sense organs and a mouth.

The skin of a roundworm is tough and bendable, but it does not grow. Young roundworms have to shed their skins, or **molt,** as they grow bigger. A roundworm molts four times between hatching and becoming an adult.

Roundworms on plants

Many different kinds of roundworms live on plants. Most have a sharp spike called a stylet, which is part of their mouth. Roundworms use it to pierce the tough outer walls of plant **cells,** then they suck out the insides.

Soil roundworms

Many different kinds of roundworms live in the soil. Some eat **bacteria,** others eat **fungi,** and still others are **predators** on other roundworms. They play an important part in breaking down dead material and releasing **nutrients** that help plants to grow. They are also food for bigger animals such as insects.

Plant Parasites

Many kinds of **microbes** live on plants. Some cause their host plant no harm, but others can cause diseases. **Fungi** are the most common disease producers.

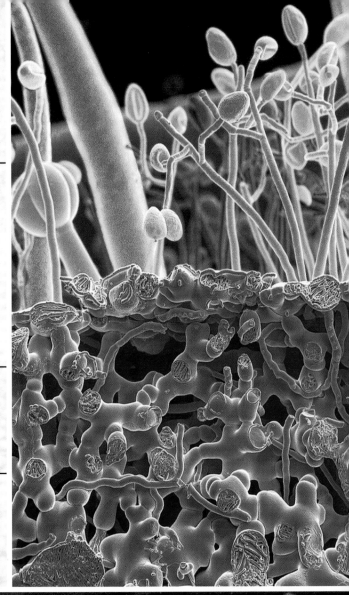

*This is part of a potato leaf with **blight** (x252). The stalks with oval pods on the end are the fungus's spore-producing bodies. Threadlike **hyphae** are visible inside the leaf tissue.*

*This photo shows **leaf spot** on a begonia leaf. Only the spore-producing bodies (the white spots) can be seen at the surface.*

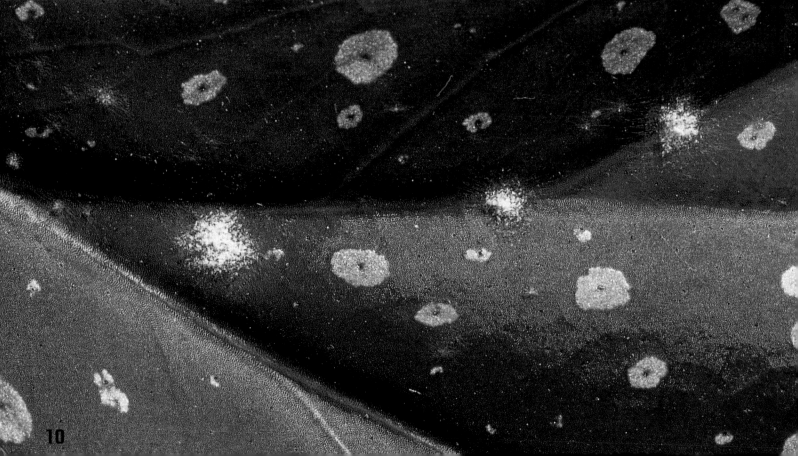

What are fungi?

Mushrooms are the best-known kinds of fungi, but there are many others. Some grow in the soil, others live on dead plants or animals, and still others are **parasites.** Fungi grow in one place and do not move around. They do not make their own food as plants do. Instead they grow on or into their food and absorb **nutrients** from it.

Fungi reproduce by making microscopic seeds called **spores.** Some fungi produce light, dry spores that can be spread by the slightest breeze. Others produce wet spores, which trickle away into the soil or onto other parts of a plant.

Getting a foothold

When a spore lands on a plant, if conditions are right, it will begin to grow. Often, the spore cannot get through the plant's thick outer waxy layer, so a tube grows along the surface. Plants have many tiny holes in them, which allow them to breathe. If the tube

WHY HIDDEN LIFE?

Mushrooms are not microscopic, so why do we call fungi hidden life? The part of a fungus that we normally see—a mushroom or a bracket fungus, for instance—is not its body, but the structure that produces spores. The main body of the fungus is made up of microscopic threads called hyphae. The hyphae are hidden in the soil, leaf, or whatever the fungus is growing on.

from a spore finds one of these holes, it grows down it and into the plant.

Different diseases

Different fungi cause different diseases in plants. Powdery **mildews** grow on the plant surface and produce spores that are like fine powder. Other fungi grow in small areas inside the plant, causing diseases such as leaf spot and **canker**. Some fungi affect the roots, causing **wilt.** Others affect the whole plant, which causes blight and other diseases.

Below is a magnified view (x280) of a cluster of spore-producing bodies bursting out through the surface of a leaf. This fungus causes a disease called rust.

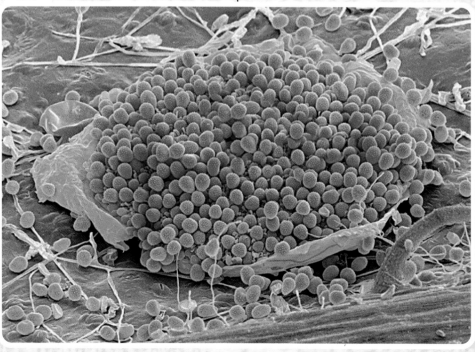

Underground Partnerships

Not all microbes that live on plants cause disease. Some work in partnership with plants. The microbes help the plants to get nutrients and water from the soil. In return, the microbes get a free supply of food. This kind of helpful partnership is called **symbiosis.**

Although plants can make their own food, they need to take up water and some **nutrients** from the soil. These nutrients are simple chemicals that plants need to grow properly. Plants often team up with **microbes** to help them get water and nutrients. Most often the partnership is with **fungi.**

🔄 *Mycorrhizal fungi spread out from tree roots over a wide area. Many are mushroom-type fungi.*

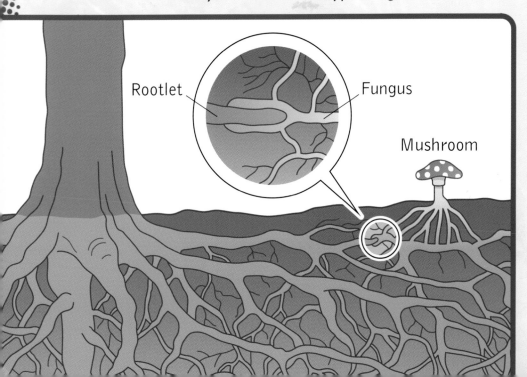

Rootlet

Fungus

Mushroom

Fungus roots

Most plants have one or more types of fungi living in or around their roots. The combination is called a **mycorrhiza** (my-cor-iza), which means "fungus root."

As we saw on page 11, the body of a fungus is made up of microscopic threads called **hyphae.** In a mycorrhiza, these hyphae

This cep, or "penny bun," is the fruiting body (the **spore**-producing part) of a mycorrhizal fungus.

and turn it into ammonia, a very important nutrient for plants. In return, the bacteria are able to feed on sugars produced by the plant.

With *Rhizobium* bacteria in their roots, legumes can grow in soils that other plants cannot survive in.

Rhizobium *bacteria can live independently in the soil, or they can grow in a plant's roots.*

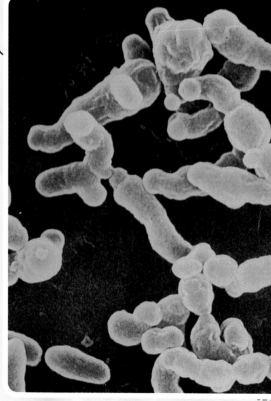

spread out from the plant's roots and greatly increase the area of soil from which the plant can absorb nutrients. In return for help in getting water and nutrients, the plant supplies the fungus with some of the sugary food that it makes.

Mycorrhizas are most important for trees, but they are found in most kinds of plants. Some plants cannot survive without fungi growing on their roots. Others grow more slowly if they have no fungi.

Peas and beans

Another kind of partnership is important for legumes (plants such as peas, beans, and peanuts). These plants form partnerships with **bacteria** called *Rhizobium.* These bacteria can take **nitrogen** gas from the air

Microlife in the Soil

Every handful of garden soil is full of microlife. These microscopic creatures do a very important job. They are nature's cleanup squad. They break down fallen leaves, animal wastes, dead insects, and other materials and turn them into rich soil.

Imagine what would happen if dead animals, animal wastes, and dead plants did not **decompose.** In a very short time the world would be swamped with waste materials. The process of getting rid of nature's waste happens in the soil. Every teaspoon of soil is full of life, and nearly all of it is very tiny.

Breaking up the waste

Before **microbes** can get to work, earthworms, beetles, and other soil minibeasts have to break up nature's wastes into smaller pieces. When a tree dies, for instance, all kinds of beetles and other insects tunnel into the dead wood. Birds such as woodpeckers also make holes as they dig into the wood looking for insects. The tunnels and holes made by these animals allow other insects, **roundworms,** and **fungi** to get into the wood.

Earthworms and other minibeasts are important in the first stage of breaking down natural wastes.

In a similar way, leaves, smaller plants, and animal wastes are broken into pieces by earthworms and insects. This is an important step because it helps microbes get at the wastes and speeds up decomposition. Earthworms are the most important of the large decomposers. All the soil you have ever seen has passed through the stomachs of several earthworms.

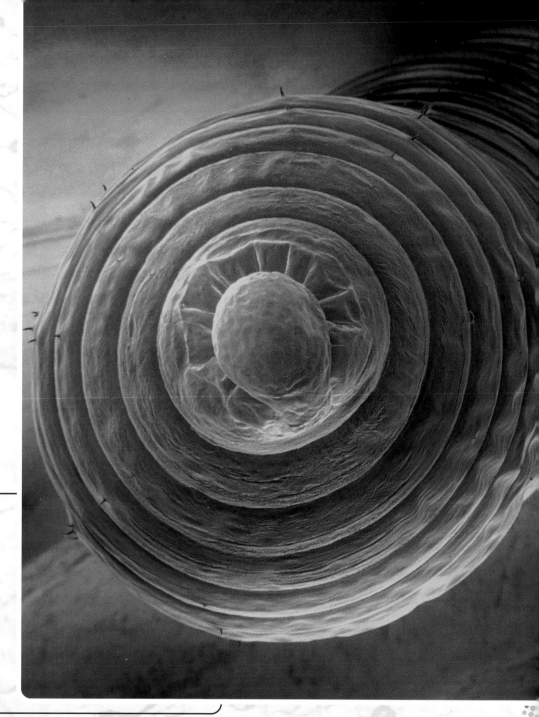

At right is an earthworm's head enlarged 72 times. Earthworms take in huge amounts of soil and get food from it. The waste comes out as worm casts, which are tiny piles of fine dirt.

A TEASPOON OF SOIL

teaspoon of rich soil contains an incredible number of creatures. These include:
- one or two smaller insects such as springtails
- up to 5,000 roundworms
- up to 100,000 algae (plantlike **microbes)**
- anything from a few thousand to 2½ million fungi
- up to 4 billion bacteria

A teaspoon of soil is too small to contain any earthworms, but 2.5 acres (1 hectare) contains up to 3 million of them.

The Decomposers

Once natural waste materials have been broken up into pieces, the **decomposers** can get to work. The most important decomposers are **fungi** and **bacteria.**

Soil bacteria

Bacteria are found throughout the soil. They live in thin films of water that cling to soil particles. Different bacteria can use a wide range of substances as food. Some live on materials such as **proteins** that are made by living things. Some can use the waste products from other bacteria as food. Some can use **nitrogen** from the air to help them get energy. Others can live without any air—they do not need to breathe.

The overall result of the activity of all these bacteria is that natural wastes are broken down, and **nutrients** that plants can use are released into the soil.

These Bacillus bacteria (x2723) are common on decomposing material. Each type of decomposing bacteria can break down different types of chemicals.

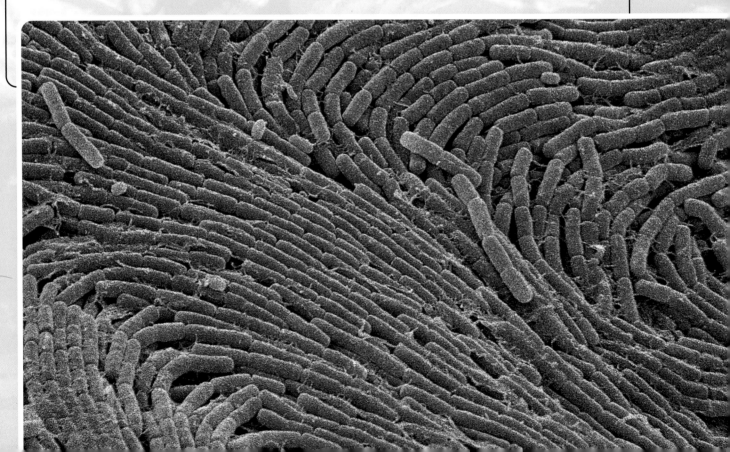

contain a tough material called lignin. Bacteria usually have no effect on lignin, but fungi can break it down.

Fungi are also more active than bacteria in acid soils. Many bacteria cannot grow in acidic conditions, but fungi can. Forest soils tend to be acidic, and they contain a lot of woody material, so fungi are often the main decomposers in forests.

Breaking down natural wastes is not the only job that soil **bacteria** do. Many produce a sticky slime, which helps to bind tiny soil particles together into bigger particles. This helps keep the soil moist and airy, which is good for growing plants.

Soil fungi

Although bacteria are the most important decomposers, there are some jobs that **fungi** are better at. Woody plants and trees

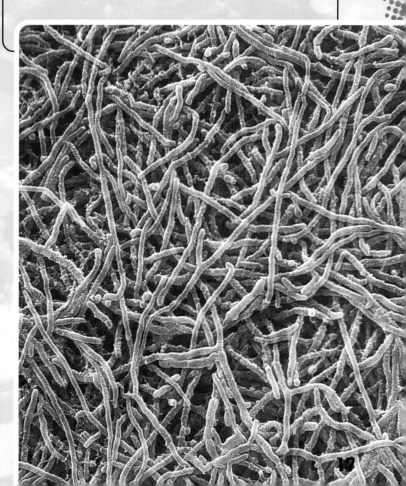

HUMONGOUS FUNGUS

Single **hyphae** of fungi are microscopic, but all the hyphae together from a single fungus can cover a huge area. One *Armillaria* fungus in a forest in Oregon covers an area of nearly square miles (10 square kilometers).

Microscopic Grazers

Decomposers are not the only microscopic creatures in the soil. There are also **microbes** that graze on **bacteria** and **fungi.** Without these grazers, the decomposers would grow out of control.

Some **roundworms** are microscopic grazers. There are also single-celled creatures called **protozoans** and tiny minibeasts called springtails.

Protozoans

Like bacteria, protozoans are creatures that consist of only one cell. But they are bigger and more complex than bacteria. Many different kinds of protozoans live in the film of water that sticks to soil particles.

Amoebas are protozoans that can send out long, fingerlike structures called **pseudopods.** Amoebas use their pseudopods to pull themselves along or catch bacteria. Flagellates have a few long, whiplike hairs called **flagella,** which make them fast swimmers. Ciliates are covered in tiny hairs called cilia. Ciliates move by waving their **cilia.**

Vorticella (x1578) is a ciliate that lives in wet soils. Its mouth is surrounded by a ring of cilia that beat to draw in food.

The different kinds of protozoans get food in different ways. Amoebas creep along through the soil and surround prey with their pseudopods before the prey notice what is happening. Ciliates do not need to move quickly because they can use their cilia to wave a current of water and small food particles toward their mouth. Flagellates are more like hunters. They can move quickly and catch larger prey.

This is a magnified photo (x18) of a springtail.

Foraminiferans are ocean-living relatives of soil amoebas. Rocks such as chalk and limestone are made of the squashed-together shells of foraminiferans that died millions of years ago.

Springtails

Springtails are close relatives of insects that live in all kinds of soil. They are about a millimeter in length and have a variety of colors—black, gray, white, yellow, lavender, red, green, or gold. They graze on **bacteria**, fungi, and whatever other food they find.

Springtails get their name from a forked tail on the underside of their abdomen. This fork is tucked under their body like a spring. When a springtail needs to make a quick getaway, it releases the forked spring and flips itself into the air.

Like **roundworms** and protozoans, springtails help to keep the numbers of decomposing microbes under control.

Creating Compost

Does your family have a **compost** heap in the yard? It could be simply a pile of grass cuttings, weeds, and kitchen scraps. Or you might have a bin to make your compost in. Compost heaps are full of microscopic organisms. They can turn your waste into a rich, brown compost that will improve the soil.

It is important to let plenty of air into a compost heap because the quickest decomposing microbes need oxygen to live. Without air, the heap can become slimy and smelly.

Rich, brown, crumbly compost like this improves the garden soil and helps the plants to grow.

Many of the creatures in a compost heap are **decomposers** from the soil. They get into the compost on plants that are put into the heap. But a compost heap is more concentrated than normal soil, so things happen differently.

Heating up

When you first start a compost heap, the material decomposes quite slowly. But as the amount of waste grows, a huge number of decomposers form, and they generate a lot of heat. The compost may get so hot that it gives off steam.

Such temperatures are too high for most **microbes.** But some kinds of **bacteria** love hot conditions, and they flourish when the temperature rises.

At high temperatures the chemical changes in the heap happen much faster, so the compost decomposes more quickly.

Cooling down

After a few months, most of the material in the compost has been broken down and the heap begins to cool. Larger decomposers now move in, such as earthworms, woodlice, and mushrooms. During this stage the compost becomes darker and more crumbly.

Keeping it cool

Compost heaps do not always get hot. Sometimes the heap remains cool, perhaps because of the type of waste or because the weather is cold. The pile of waste still turns into compost, but the process takes much longer.

One bad thing about cool composting is that it does not kill the seeds of weeds. This means that weeds that are producing seeds cannot be put into the heap because the seeds will grow when the compost is put in the garden.

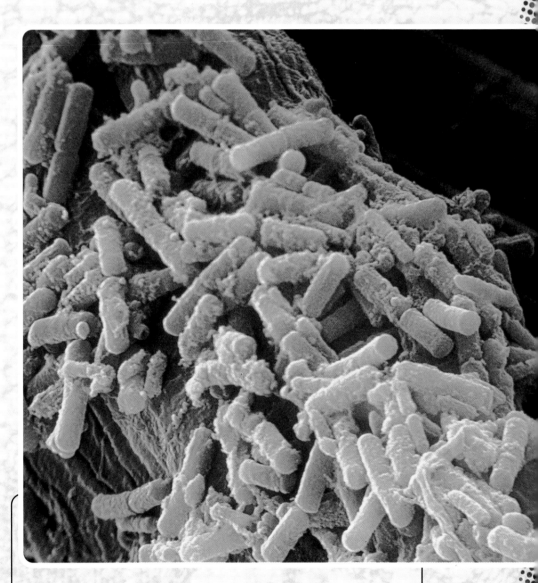

Heat-loving bacteria like Bacillus Stearothermophilus *grow best at temperatures of 130 – 160 °F.*

Water Life

You may have a pond in your yard. If not, you might have a birdbath, a rain barrel, or just a muddy puddle. Often the water looks greenish or has a green slime on it. These are signs of hidden life.

These rocklike lumps started life as colonies of **cyanobacteria** like the kind that grow in your garden. But over millions of years they have hardened into large **fossils.**

The spiral **chloroplasts** of Spirogyra run through each cell. The **cells** are joined end to end to form long strings.

Some of the **microbes** in water are like plants—they can make food by **photosynthesis.** Such microbes begin to appear in water almost as soon as it collects. They may be blown through the air and land in the water, or they may come from the soil.

Desmids can be found in ponds, puddles, gutters— anywhere where there is fresh water.

The tiniest "plants"

The tiniest microbes that can photosynthesize are called cyanobacteria. They are usually blue-green because they contain a blue-green pigment, or coloring, that helps them get energy from light. However, some cyanobacteria are red or pink because they contain other pigments that hide the blue-green color. Red cyanobacteria might turn the water in your birdbath red!

Algae

The other plantlike microbes in water are larger living things known as **algae.** There are many different kinds. Some join together in a long string, while others are single cells freely swimming in the water.

One of the most common algae to grow in strings is *Spirogyra.* Like plants and other algae, *Spirogyra* have tiny green structures called chloroplasts in their cells. Most chloroplasts are oval, but in *Spirogyra* they are long spirals.

Among the most beautiful of the free-swimming algae are microscopic green jewels known as desmids. Desmids are made up of two half-cells joined in the middle. Each half-cell is a mirror image of the other.

Algae and cyanobacteria can be a source of food for other water creatures. But if they grow unchecked, they can block the light and use up the oxygen in the water so that other water plants cannot grow.

More Water Life

The plantlike microbes in water provide food for other microlife. There are protozoans that look like tiny suns, very small animals with wheel-like structures, and relatives of crabs that serve as fish food.

The **protozoans** in water include amoebas, ciliates, and flagellates similar to those found in soil. Relatives of amoebas called actinopods also live in water.

Ray feet

Actinopods are round, with many thin rays projecting from their bodies like the rays of the sun. These rays are similar to the **pseudopods** of amoebas.

Actinopods use these spiky pseudopods to gather food. **Microbes** get tangled in the mass of spikes, and the actinopod then releases chemicals that break down the food.

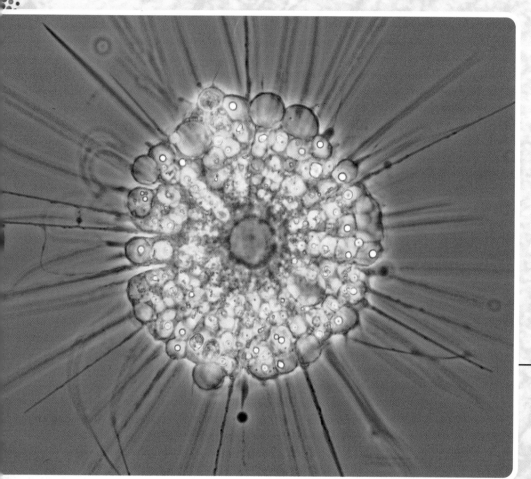

Spinning wheels

Wherever there is fresh water, you are likely to find rotifers. These tiny creatures get their name from one or more wheellike crowns of tiny moving hairs called **cilia** on their bodies. A wave of movement runs around this wheel of cilia, making it look as if the wheel is rotating.

The group of actinopods found in fresh water are called Heliozoa, which means "sun animals."

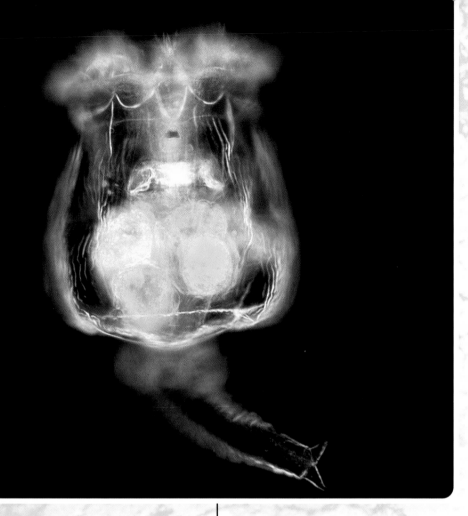

Water fleas are not insects. They are **crustaceans,** animals related to crabs. They are called fleas because of the way they seem to hop through the water. They are about 0.08 inch (2 mm) long and see-through.

The most common water fleas are called *Daphnia.* They eat mainly bacteria and small algae. Other kinds of water fleas are predators. They tear pieces out of their victim's body with their strong jaws.

If the water a rotifer (x105) is living in dries out, the rotifer dries into a wrinkled speck. But some rotifers can survive drying out and become active when water becomes available.

Daphnia *are water fleas. They are an important ingredient in goldfish food sold in pet shops.*

Rotifers can use their wheels to move through the water or to wave food into their mouths. Some rotifers graze on **algae** or **bacteria**, but others are fierce **predators.** One kind of rotifer eats water fleas.

Water fleas

You can find water fleas in almost any patch of water.

Two-in-One Creatures

Are there patches of color on the rocks or trees in your yard? If so, they might be lichens. Lichens grow in all kinds of places, from burning deserts to the freezing Antarctic. Although they grow like plants, lichens are actually an amazing **symbiosis**—fungi and algae living together in partnership.

Most of a lichen is fungus, but living among the threads of the fungus are one-celled photosynthesizers—either **algae** or **cyanobacteria.** These **cells** can make their own food. In return for protection and support, they share this food with the fungus part of the lichen.

Types of lichens

There are more than 16,000 kinds of lichens, each one a combination of a different **fungus** and alga. Some lichens grow as a crust on surfaces. Some look like pebbles or have a leafy appearance, and some are branchlike.

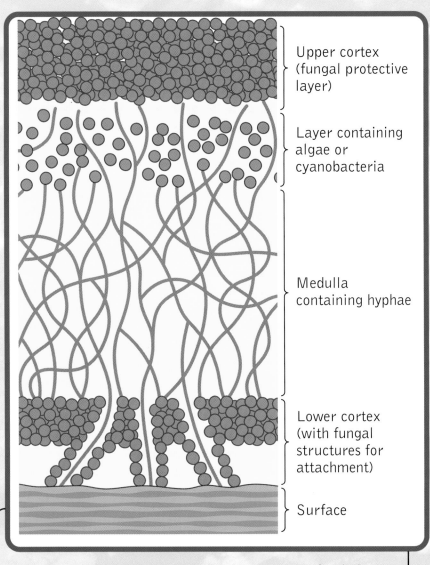

Upper cortex (fungal protective layer)

Layer containing algae or cyanobacteria

Medulla containing hyphae

Lower cortex (with fungal structures for attachment)

Surface

This diagram shows the layered structure of a lichen: the top and bottom layers are made of fungus cells (brown), while the middle layer is composed of hyphae (brown threads) and alga cells (green).

All lichens are basically alike. The outer layer is made up of tightly packed fungus cells, which protect the lichen. In the next layer, alga cells are scattered among the fungus's **hyphae.** Below this is a third layer of fungus cells, which attaches the lichen to the surface it grows on.

Sensitive survivors

Lichens are able to survive in places where fungi or algae alone cannot. The algae make food for the fungus by **photosynthesis,** so the lichen does not need a food source. And the fungus protects the algae from drying out, which means that lichens can survive in dry places.

Although lichens are tough, many kinds are sensitive to pollution. Only a few types of lichens grow in cities because most are killed by pollution in the air.

Crustose lichen is one of the few lichens that can survive in towns and cities.

BEATRIX POTTER'S IDEA

Beatrix Potter, who wrote *Peter Rabbit* and other children's books, studied the idea that lichens were partnerships of two different living things. Potter was an excellent student of nature, and her drawings of fungi and lichens are still admired today. However, her discoveries about lichens were not recognized during her lifetime.

Table of Sizes

Although all hidden life is tiny, there is a huge range of sizes.
To a flea, a grain of pollen seems just as tiny as the flea seems to us.

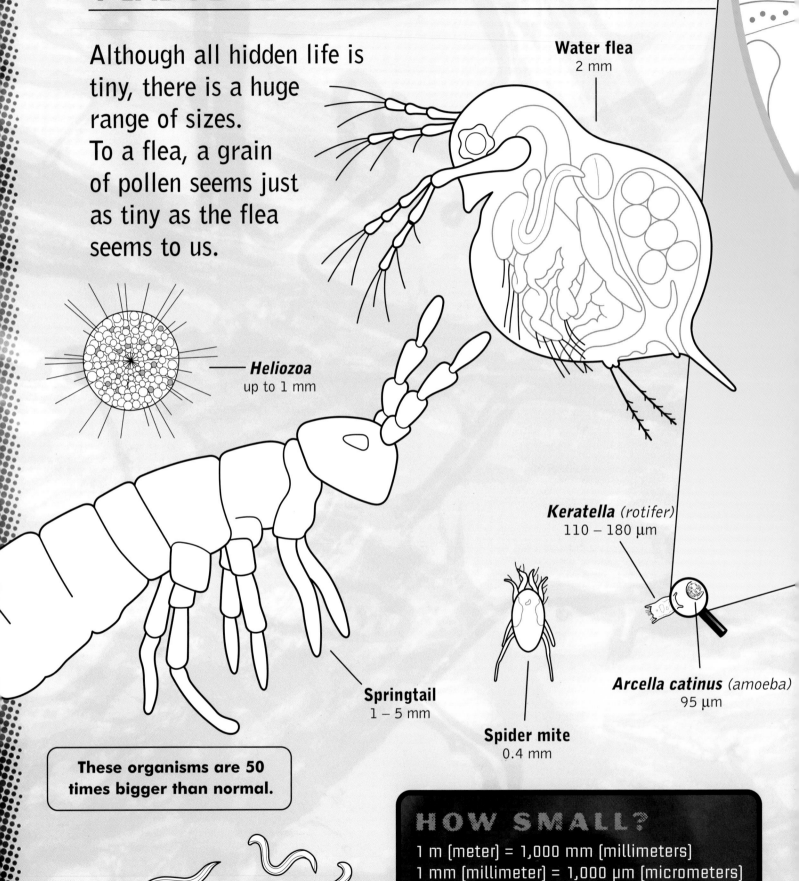

Water flea
2 mm

Heliozoa
up to 1 mm

Keratella (rotifer)
110 – 180 µm

Arcella catinus (amoeba)
95 µm

Springtail
1 – 5 mm

Spider mite
0.4 mm

These organisms are 50 times bigger than normal.

Roundworms
1 mm

HOW SMALL?

1 m (meter) = 1,000 mm (millimeters)
1 mm (millimeter) = 1,000 µm (micrometers)
1 µm (micrometer) = 1,000 nm (nanometers)

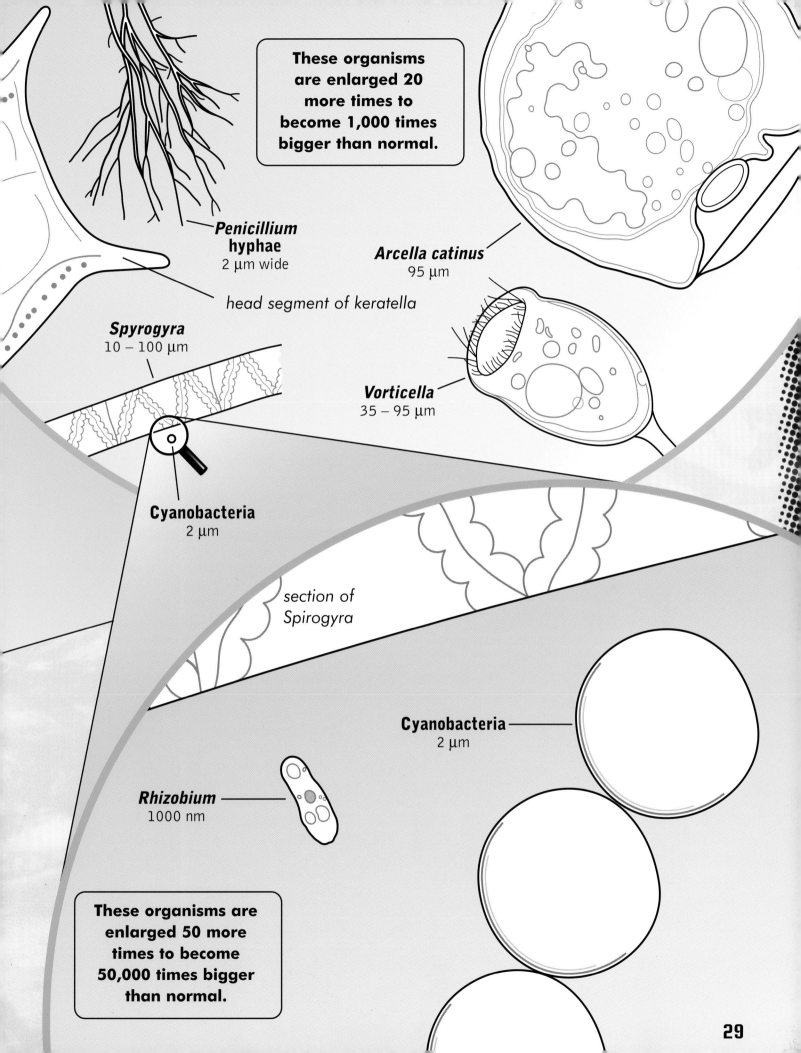

These organisms are enlarged 20 more times to become 1,000 times bigger than normal.

Penicillium
hyphae
2 µm wide

Arcella catinus
95 µm

head segment of keratella

Spyrogyra
10 – 100 µm

Vorticella
35 – 95 µm

Cyanobacteria
2 µm

section of
Spirogyra

Cyanobacteria
2 µm

Rhizobium
1000 nm

These organisms are enlarged 50 more times to become 50,000 times bigger than normal.

29

Glossary

acid   substance that is sour, sharp, or able to dissolve other substances. Lemon juice and vinegar are acids.

algae   plantlike living things, most of which are microscopic. Only one of these organisms is called an alga.

bacteria   microscopic living things, each one only a single cell. They are different from other one-celled creatures because they do not have a nucleus. Only one of these living things is called a bacterium.

blight   fungus disease affecting the whole plant

canker   plant disease that causes wounds, or cankers, on the roots, stem, or branches

cells   building blocks of living things. Some living things are single cells, while others are made up of billions of cells working together.

chloroplasts   tiny parts within plant cells that turn light energy into food

cilia   tiny hairlike structures that stick out from the surface of some microbes. They can beat together in a rhythm to move the microbe along or wave food toward it. A cilium is a single one of these structures.

compost   brown, crumbly material made of decayed plant wastes. Compost is used to enrich soil.

crustaceans   large group of animals that includes crabs, shrimps, lobsters, and water fleas

cyanobacteria   bacteria that can make their own food from light, water, and carbon dioxide, as plants can do

decompose   to break down chemically, or rot

electron microscope   very powerful microscope that can magnify objects up to 500,000 times

flagella   long, whiplike hairs that can move from side to side. A flagellum is a single one of these hairs.

fossil   remains or the impression of a long-dead organism in rock

fungus   plantlike living thing such as a mushroom or a yeast. Two or more of these organisms are called fungi.

hibernation   to go into an inactive state to cope with unpleasant environmental conditions

hyphae   thin, threadlike cells that make up the body of most fungi. A hypha is a single one of these cells.

leaf spot   fungus infection on plants that shows up as spots on leaves

larva   young stage of some types of insects. A larva looks different from an adult and has to go through a changing stage (the pupa) in order to become an adult.

mammal   warm-blooded, hairy or furry animal that feeds its young on milk

microbe   microscopic creature such as a bacterium, algae, protozoan, or virus

mildew   type of fungus that infects plants and shows as a powdery or soft fuzzy covering on affected parts of the plant

mite   tiny, round-bodied creature with eight legs that is closely related to spiders

molt   to shed hair, feathers, or skin. When an insect molts, it sheds its hard outer skeleton in order to grow.

mycorrhiza   plant roots with fungi growing around or into them, where the fungi help absorb nutrients and water from the soil and get food from the plant in return

nitrogen   colorless gas with no smell

nutrients   chemicals that nourish living things

nymph   temporary immature form of some insects

parasite   creature that lives on or in another living creature and takes its food from it, without giving any benefit in return and often causing harm

photosynthesis   process by which plants make sugars (food) from carbon dioxide, water, and light energy

predator   animal that hunts and kills another animal for food.

protein   substance used to build structures within living things and to control the thousands of chemical reactions that happen inside cells

protozoan   one-celled creature that has larger, more complicated cells than bacteria

pseudopod   fingerlike structure that an amoeba sends out to move around and catch food. The word means "false foot."

roundworm   a type of mostly small, simple worm that is found in large numbers in just about every environment on Earth

spore   very tiny seedlike structure that a fungus uses to reproduce. A bacterial spore is a bacterium that has formed a tough outer coat to help it survive difficult conditions.

springtail small, six-legged creature closely related to insects that are found in the soil

stylet sharp, pointed spike that is part of the mouth of many plant-eating minibeasts

symbiosis partnership between two living things in which both creatures benefit

wilt plant disease that causes the plant to droop from lack of water

More Books to Read

Editorial staff. *Microscopic Investigations: Plant Biology.* Vernon Hills, Ill.: Learning Resources, 2001.

Lavies, Bianca. *Compost Critters.* New York: Penguin Putnam Books for Young Readers, 2001.

McGinty, Alice B. *Decomposers in the Food Chain.* New York: Rosen Publishing Group, 2002.

Miles Kelly Staff. *Larger Than Life: Gigantic Views of the Microscopic.* Chicago: Independent Publishers Group, 2003.

Snedden, Robert. *Cells and Life: The Diversity of Life.* Chicago: Heinemann Library, 2002.

Ward, Brian R. *Microscopic Life in the Garden.* North Mankato, Minn.: Smart Apple Media, 2004.

Index

Actinomycetes 17
actinopods 24
algae 15, 23, 26, 27, 28
ammonia 13
amoebas 18, 19, 24, 28

Bacillus 16
Bacillus stearothermophilus 21
bacteria 9, 13, 15, 28
   cyanobacteria 22, 23, 26, 28
   decomposers 16–17
   heat-loving bacteria 21
   soil bacteria 16–17
   waste products 16
blight 10, 11

Caenorhabditis elegans 9
canker 11
cells
   microbes 18, 23
   plant cells 7, 9
chloroplasts 22, 23
ciliates 18, 19, 24, 28
compost 20–1
crustaceans 25
Crustose lichen 27
cyanobacteria 22, 23, 26, 28

Daphnia 25
decomposers 18, 19, 20, 21
   bacteria 16–17
   earthworms 15, 21
   fungi 14, 17, 21
   roundworms 9, 14
decomposition 14–17
desmids 23, 28

earthworms 5, 8, 14, 15, 21
eggs 7
electron microscope 5

flagellates 18, 19, 24

foraminiferans 19
fossils 22
fungi 5, 9, 10-11, 14, 15, 28
   decomposers 17, 21
   hyphae 11, 12–13
   lichens 26, 27
   mycorrhizal fungi 12–13
   soil fungi 17
   spores 11

grazers 18–19

Heliozoa 24, 28
hibernation 7

larvae 7
leaf spot 10, 11
legumes 13
lichens 26–7
lignin 17

microbes 5
   microscopic grazers 18–19
   symbiosis 12–13
   water life 22–3
   see also algae; bacteria; fungi; protozoans
microscopes 5
   electron microscope 5
   light microscope 5
mildews 11
mites 4, 28
   predatory mites 7
   red mites 6
   spider mites 6–7, 28
   stylets 7

nitrogen 13, 16
nutrients 5, 9, 11, 12, 13, 16
nymphs 7

parasites
   fungi 10-11
   roundworms 8
photosynthesis 23, 26, 27
plant pests and diseases 5, 6–7, 8, 10, 11

pollution 27
potato blight 10
Potter, Beatrix 27
predators
   mites 7
   rotifers 25
   roundworms 9
   water fleas 25
proteins 16
protozoans 18, 24
   amoebas 18, 19, 24
   ciliates 18, 19, 24, 28
   flagellates 18, 19, 24

red mites 6
Rhizobium 13, 28
rotifers 24–5, 28
roundworms 4, 8-9, 14, 15, 28
   grazers 18
   plant roundworms 8, 9
   predatory roundworms 9
   soil roundworms 8, 9
   stylets 9
rust 11

soil 5, 9, 14–15
   acid soil 17
   soil bacteria 16–17
   soil fungi 17
spider mites 6–7, 28
Spirogyra 22, 23, 28
spores 11
springtails 15, 18, 19, 28
symbiosis 12–13, 26

Vorticella 18, 28

water fleas 25, 28
water life 22–5
weed seeds 21
wilt 11
woodlice 21
worms
   earthworms 5, 8, 14, 15, 21
   roundworms 4, 8–9, 14, 15, 18, 28
   worm casts 15